AWAY WITH WORDS

Young Writers' 16th Annual Poetry Competition

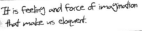

It is feeling and force of imagination that make us eloquent.

How can I not dream while writing? The blank page gives a right to dream.

YoungWriters

Cardiff

Edited by Allison Dowse

Contents

Radyr Comprehensive School

Emily Bright (13)   76
Alex Coombes (13)   77
Minh-Tri Lam (13)   78
Pritesh Varsani (13)   79
Vaughan Kenward (13)   80
Jack Shellard (13)   81
Laura Green (11)   82
Hannah Dykes (11)   83
Sophie Shenton (11)   84
Sophie Austin (11)   85
Briony Powell (12)   86
Emma Williams (12)   87
Sophia Homayoonfar (13)   88
Lydia Le Saux (13)   89
Laura Burford (13)   90
Thomas Spiteri (12)   91
Cherie Roberts (12)   92
Laura Anderton (13)   93
Michael Flowers (12)   94
Marc Davies (13)   95
Adam Pincombe (12)   96
Oliver Haines (12)   97
Sarah Carroll (12)   98
Luke Gilbert (12)   99
Perry Rowlands (12)   100
Roseanne Payne (14)   101

Ysgol Gyfun Gymraeg Plasmawr

Kate Anderson (12)   102
Ffion Wright (13)   103
Cerys Lane (12)   104
Anders Roblin (13)   105
Indeg Williams (12)   106
Anna Williams (13)   107
Angharad Rosser (12)   108
Caio Redknap (12)   109
Jordan Walcott (13)   110
Louis Uncles (13)   111
Taylor Brady (13)   112
Matthew Lewis (13)   113
Daniel Khan (14)   114

The Poems

Justice

Occurs when both parties feel equal
And can come together
Like negative and positive
And be as one.

It can bring vengeful satisfaction
Over cruel villains
And it cuts like a knife
To defend the innocent
Which blindingly appears
To be a solution.

Justice is the proving right
When everyone said
It was wrong
And being able to be
Contempt.

Linley Hermance (17)
Cardiff Centre of Excellence

Joy

Joy is a mother's face with her first child
It is a river of endless love
Happiness is a trail of beloved memories
Which flow like a river in the mind's eye

And the brain holds the memories of joy
With a feeling that imposes lightness
In our special, precious closet of experience.

Hiral Narbad-Shah (14)
Cardiff Centre of Excellence

For You

I wrote a song for you
But I threw it in the trash

I wrote a letter to you
But I hid it in my stash

I drew a picture for you
But I gave it to a friend

I wrote a song for you
But I erased it in the end

I had a dream for you
But when I woke up I forgot

I made a wish for you
But I make that wish a lot

I could say I never hoped for 'us'
But then I would have lied

I always wanted 'us' together . . .
But I guess I never tried.

Jane Motley (14)
Cardiff High School

70 Miles Away

Very long journey
Going down to Nan's
Not long left now
70 miles away

Can't wait to get there
Haven't seen her in a while
Not long left now
50 miles away

Starting to get bored now
Sitting in this car
Not long left now
30 miles away

Getting very close
I can see the sea
Not long left now
10 miles away

Pulling up in front of her house
She's waiting outside for me
Finally here, I'm stepping out the car
'Wow,' she says, 'look how tall you are!'

Scott Franklin (14)
Cardiff High School

Toasting The Bride

She came out from her ordeal
Burned and scathed.
Her dress was singed,
Her hair a mess,
I don't suppose she was impressed.
We were just reliving a wedding tradition,
The toasting of the bride.

Suzie Harris (14)
Cardiff High School

A Semi-Detached With A Turquoise Door

A semi-detached with a turquoise door
Frosted with snow the window's complete.
Laughter, music tickles my ears.

Frosted with snow the window's complete.
A semi-detached with a turquoise door
Soft, fluffy fur brings comfort.

Laughter, music tickles my ears
Frosted with snow the windows complete
Happy, relaxed, safe in the home.

Soft, fluffy fur brings comfort
A semi-detached with a turquoise door
Warm, cosy bed inside the cocoon.

Jenny Drage (15)
Cardiff High School

The City

A crowded city centre
A wild beating heart
Django Reinhardt twists and turns
Linking up its parts

The deserted little alleys
A forgotten urban park
The tree a hundred times my age
Graffiti lines its bark

And when I think I've lost it all
A knock comes at my door
On the doorstep stands the city
And it's always wanting more.

Will Evans (15)
Cardiff High School

Seek For You

I seek for you in deepest part of the lake,
I seek for you every minute of every day,
In the corner of every room,
At the tallest part of every tower,
I seek for you,
I seek for you at dawn,
I seek for you at dusk,
I listen to my heart,
It tells me I must,
In the blizzard and
In the draught
I continue to seek when no one's about
The day will come when I stop my search
My soul will bleed,
Yet you continue to lurch,
In the shadows,
In the darkness of the night.

Harriet Chapman (15)
Cardiff High School

The Anti-Sonnet Sonnet

My love for sonnets is non-existent
My mind is full of better things to do
I sit down to write with no true intent
Although it is strange it is rather true
When I really do try to write sonnets
And I ready myself to do the work
They always end up with some of my wits
In the back of my mind the sonnets lurk
I try to find them but with no success
When I find them, they come out all wrong
And the blank white page becomes a dark mess
And when I say them they become a song
Even this sonnet is starting to suck
I will try again and hope for more luck.

David Roberts (14)
Cardiff High School

Fear

Wind howling through the trees
Slanting the rain into my face
Pecan trees shaking their fruit
To make loud thumps on the ground
Like a giant's footsteps

Lightning flashes, followed by thunder
Illuminating everything and nothing
The pecan trees shaking their fruit
And making ink black shadows
For anything to hide.

Enfys O'Doherty (14)
Cardiff High School

Lock, Stock And One Smoking Barrel

It's a live destroyer
It's a course of power
It's a family protector
It's a hero maker
It's an old timer
It's an argument ender
It's a devil servant,
It's a pistol,
A pistol,
A pistol.

David Lloyd-Williams (15)
Cardiff High School

Big White House Of Wonders

Sandy brown boulders surround
A big white house of wonders
Like the hot African sun that burns my soul

A big white house of wonders
Lost without its sandy brown boulders
Welcome the hysterical calling of children to their father

The hot African sun that burns my soul
Lingers around the big white house of wonders
Distressing the soft silk crimson soil

Hysterical calling of children to their father
Destroys the sandy brown boulders
So I feel no pain no fear just memories and comfort to my heart.

Babongile Ndiweni (15)
Cardiff High School

A Journey

The oar dipping in time
In and out of the chilled water
The kayak swinging from side to side
Like a baby in a cradle

Small water boatmen boating around
Green water weeds grabbing at the oar
The bright sky reflecting on the surface
Glistening and shimmering in the motion.

Little birds, preen in the shade
Delicately perching on the branches,
Overhanging on the surface,
As we continue our journey downstream.

With our arms tied,
And bodies aching,
We make the final strokes with effort,
The finish life is in sight.

Anna Jezierska (15)
Cardiff High School

I Remember Now

The leaves flutter around the trees
Wraith-like, they make their descent
Slowly settling,
The wet grass seeps through my jeans,
The mud congeals on my hands,
I take a quick breath,
The cold air burns my throat and lungs,
The oppressive darkness is all around,
And whispers scatter through the fields,
But I don't care,
It is perfect,
I remember now,
What I had not,
For memories, like those words
Can hurt.

Huw Fullerton (14)
Cardiff High School

Foot In One's Mouth

Conversation buzzes with excitement
Voices get louder as each one competes
No one's getting heard
Each person only interested in themselves
I sit, taking each sentence in
As each comment comes, a bad feeling grows bigger
Knowing I won't be able to handle many more,
My mouth opens wide,
Words spill out rapidly filling the room,
Unable to stop the fast flow, I watch words flitter about
In front of me.
My leg jerks forward and before I can stop it
My foot bends to face me.
Silence falls upon the room
The intense stare from the crowd digs into me
As my mouth reopens my foot climbs in without struggling for space
I hobble around on one leg
Now knowing, I have put my foot in my mouth.

Anna Gasson (15)
Cardiff High School

His Heart

His heart ablaze, raring through the night
Growing larger by each second, each breath
A deep mysterious stare, peeking through the light
The fire concealed, waiting for the lover's death
At its full pace, glazing under the moon
Still with a roar, he remains at doubt
The ravenous flames, anticipating for the soon
His heart ablaze, only she can put it out.

His heart a seed, the dream of development controls him
All alone with just the thoughts, the nightmare of his break
Trying to reach out, a failure, lying is a helpless limb
After a while, could this be his time? A new mind forms in its wake.
Three gentle words, a saved life, a saved soul
And if the truth, their hearts would bind so strong
His need for love and care, the spark that would make him whole
His heart a seed, growing old with her is where they belong.

Carly Johnson (16)
Cardiff High School

Quietly In The Sun

I push open the gate cautiously,
The gate to a world of serenity.
I make my way through nature's beauties,
Swaying grass and scattered poppies.
I breathe deeply, taking in the fresh country air,
Filling my body with a new lease of life.

I sit myself down under a single oak tree,
The only noise the slight rustling of grass.
I sit like this, quietly in the sun,
Until there is nothing more to see.
I sit like this under the moonlight, wondering
How I didn't notice something so beautiful,
Slipping away so quickly.

Charlotte Sewell (14)
Cardiff High School

The Penguin

It can taste the soft snow,
It can feel the Arctic winds blow,
It can explore the vast sea,
Underwater, it's free.

But it can't fly away,
On the ground it will stay,
They will huddle together,
As they'll seem cold forever.

They see global warming:
The icebergs deforming,
As their home disappears,
They weep frozen tears.

The fish they so cherish,
On the land, they do perish,
A meal time gone by;
'Satisfied,' they lie.

Thomas Williams (14)
Cardiff High School

Surreal

I stand astounded
Slope behind,
As my skis clip on and my goggles slip down

Slowly, silently
My skis slide up
Quickly gaining speed, as others shoot on by

I turn left, right
Wind rushes out of my face
As I suck in carbon dioxide and air is forced out

Suddenly my knees bend
And I spring into the air
Landing perfectly on the top of a snow-white jump

And when I reach the top
Desperate for more
The lift takes me down, ready for another surreal run.

Mark Harwood (14)
Cardiff High School

A Wolf In Sheep's Clothing

Hello farmer, hello lunch
Oh how I love to make bones crunch

Each day a cunning trick is needed
The farm's growth may be impeded

A disguise perhaps
To keep my snacks

No bleating cry, you'll hear from me
Instead a grin of wolfish glee

Among the sheep I'll feast tonight
Tomorrow, they'll be out of sight

And then I'll go for goats and all
My wolfish pride before their fall.

William Ashton (14)
Cardiff High School

Treorchi

Icily, it flows through my fingers, the blood of my country
A deep connection ties me here, always there, never-ending
A large bend in the horizon, hugging the houses below

A deep connection ties me here, always there, never-ending
Icily, it flows through my fingers, the blood of my country
The top of the valley blackens, as a sheet of rain engulfs it

A large bend in the horizon, hugging the houses below
A deep connection ties me here, always there never-ending
A towering eruption of history, in my heart, in my soul I feel it

The top of the valley blackens, as a sheet of rain engulfs it
Icily, it flows through my fingers, the blood of my country
A towering eruption of history, in my heart, in my soul I feel it.

Jezel Jones (14)
Cardiff High School

Paddington Station

The poster of flashes where audience gather
Breath rising in a sooty cloud
Trains screech as they run onstage

Breath rising in a sooty cloud
The poster flashed and audience gather
Numbers flash, people run into chaotic wonderland

Trains screech as they run on stage
Their breath rises in a sooty cloud
In an armadillo of cast iron and beams

Numbers flash, people run into chaotic wonderland
From the poster of flashes where they had gathered
Their stallions await to take them far away.

Hannah-Lily Perkin Smithies (15)
Cardiff High School

Duffryn Road

Chipped, dusty slates of smooth blue-grey
A flash of car shoots by rustling wind and roaming people
Looking around, I know and feel like home

A flash of car shoots by rustling wind and roaming people
Chipped, dusty slates of smooth blue-grey
A fine dewy mist swirls cold above velvet-green grass

Looking around I know and feel like home
A flash of car shoots by rustling wind and roaming people
A short straight of simple colour and bustling life

A fine dewy mist swirls cold above velvet-green grass
Chipped, dusty slates of smooth blue-grey
Twisted, gnarled dead, a sudden streak of ancient purple bark
Hidden amongst leafier brethren.

Rhian Evans (14)
Cardiff High School

Calm Humbugs

Beyond the little stream that runs into forest
A little village with farms and animals dotted
Fresh white houses on luscious green meadows

A little village with farms and animals dotted
Beyond the little stream that runs into forest
Like a child safe in the knowledge of home

Fresh white houses on luscious green meadow
A little village with farms and animals dotted
Cows, chickens, birds a babbling brook

Like a child safe in the knowledge of home
A little village with farms and animals dotted
The ground underneath your feet, calm humbugs.

Sophia Wigley (14)
Cardiff High School

Izmir

The icy water, like electricity through my tepid hands
The fountains, a centrepiece on the table of rising towers
A silent breeze caresses my skin in the blissful shade

The fountains, a centrepiece on the table of rising towers
The icy water like electricity through my tepid hands
A rising mass of colours around a magnificent centrepiece
Glimmering in the sun

A silent breeze caresses my skin in the blissful shade
The fountains, a centrepiece on the rising table of towers
Spraying me with a refreshing dose of icy water

A rising mass of colours around a magnificent centrepiece
Glimmering in the sun
The icy water, like electricity though my tepid hands
I gently caress the rough granite, it creates a comforting
Friction going through my skin, fuelling me.

Lloyd McNaughton (14)
Cardiff High School

Waterloo Gardens

The flowing river and the hill hidden in daisies
A streaming row of terraces face neatly fenced gardens
Birds humming, trees swaying, children playing

A streaming row of terraces face neatly fenced gardens
The flowing river and the hill hidden in daisies
Fluffy, creamy snow, layered on the ground, so peaceful, so tranquil

Birds humming, trees swaying, children playing
A streaming row of terraces face neatly fenced gardens
A warm glow inside, a happy feeling within.

Fluffy, creamy snow, layered on the ground, so peaceful, so tranquil
The flowing river and the hill hidden in daisies
A bridge over troubled water.

Kathryn Kelloway (14)
Cardiff High School

At Home

Ordinary and invisible, hidden in rows of bricks
With bubbles of laughter and an occasional shriek
I fall backwards into the welcome retreat of my own cosy bed

With bubbles of laughter and an occasional shriek
Ordinary and invisible, hidden in rows of bricks
I feel that I belong

I fall backwards into the welcome retreat of my own cosy bed
Listening to the bubbles of laughter and an occasional shriek
And outside, a few snowflakes flutter down

I feel that I belong,
Ordinary and invisible, hidden in rows of bricks
A misty fog of cold surrender surrounds the house.

Khadija Jamal (15)
Cardiff High School

Think Of My Own

Hard as I try I cannot concentrate
My mind begins to wander from the subject
That I am trying to debate
The thoughts I had I must reject

I begin to think of all my stuff
That I keep in my house
To quiet my mind is very tough
My mind roars, my lips as a mouse.

Andrew Davis (14)
Cardiff High School

A Sausage

It's a stomach filler
It's a pig killer
It's a bladder skinner
It's a pan sizzler
It's a grease spitter
It's a tasty appetiser
It's a sausage!

Ross Davies (14)
Cardiff High School

Lovers In Venice

Rushing, racing, rampaging through,
The boat cuts through the water,
Ripples, reflections, refreshing and true,
Heading into the nobleman's quarter.

Suddenly, screams, sounding strong,
Echo around the courtyard,
Scorching stares signal its wrong,
But hearts are forever being scarred.

Descending, deftly, down from above,
Her footsteps are light as a feather,
Dropping, delicately, declaring the love,
They push off to their future together.

Sian Fullerton (16)
Cardiff High School

Down The Gravelled Path

A place I will forever call home
The house I was brought up in
Memories fill every room
My home for always

Down the gravelled path
Past the lawns of daisies
Careful, don't ring the bell
Babies must be sleeping

Through the black wooden doors
Into the decorated hall
See the mirror
Look deep into yourself
Or feel the way and discover hidden talents.

Up the steep winding stairs
Like ascending into your goals
For at the head of the track
A room waits where tales are told

A place I will forever call home
The house I was brought up in
Memories fill every room
My home for always.

Ben Salamon (15)
Cardiff High School

A New Life

The boat rolled amongst the waves
Water crashing against the side
The sea collecting on the deck
In cool, clear pools

Underneath, in cramped, cold conditions
A man huddled, beneath the boards
Blankets wrapped around his shoulders
A new life ahead of him

Land is sighted far ahead
Seagulls flying overhead
Wrapped up men get out of bed
A new life to be led.

Matthew Ingrams (15)
Cardiff High School

No One At Home

Standing here, on this marble step,
I stare at the polished oak door
The bell's tune resounds through the hallway inside
And I wait

My eyes linger on the lion head knocker
Almost roaring in its golden beauty

I try to peer through the misty glass and see
Nothing
I take one last glance at the white pillars either side of me
And leave.

Chris Jones (15)
Cardiff High School

Journey Through Style

She started off a country girl
Western winds filling the skies
Singing the lines in chequered blue
Dark brown tobacco smoke filled her eyes

Then she reached her rocker phase
Drowning the neighbours in pungent rage
Outgrowing her acoustic strings
Wanting more adult things

She took time off from her rocker dreams
To realise what life really means
Restitching torn jeans, remaking old seams
Returning to her childhood dreams

After realising the discomfort of sports cars and stiletto heels
She returned to black army boots and truck wheels
Living the way she used to do
With a familiar smile and an undone shoe.

Hattie Clarke (15)
Cardiff High School

My Mind

Beyond my mind a splash of liquid
Bubbles of toxic gas
An underwater eruption
Of memories from a dark past

Broken glass sticks into its surface
Crushed by the weight of the steamroller
Whilst up above floats the dust of the future
Predicting the story of my mind.

Elizabeth Gallimore (15)
Cardiff High School

Tainted Soldier

The blood unclots and starts to become thin
The blood splatter draws together and returns to the skin
The red oil enters circulation as it rushes into the hollow
The flesh converges as the bits are retrieved from the barrow
The fragments attract, and there's a sugar rush of lead
The metal shards reform, bonds which then withdraws from the head
The skull condenses and shatters into its form
The energy flows and the neurons fire like an electric storm
The eyes reopen and the gasp is exhaled
The adrenaline rushes and he knows he's failed.

Jamie Sargant (14)
Cardiff High School

My Heaven

Feel the bedroom floor, supposed to be smooth but rough with
The sand gravelled into it from the beach
Outside, cloudless landscapes soar above with the birds
They see a small scatter of houses and bubbles of sea

Outside, cloudless landscapes soar above with the birds
Feel the bedroom floor, supposed to be smooth but rough with
The sand gravelled into it from the beach
I'm comforted with the apartness from the world

A small scatter of houses and bubbles of sea
Outside, cloudless landscapes soar above with the birds
A rainbow of sound sprinkles out laughter and waves

I'm comforted with the apartness from the world
Feel the bedroom floor, supposed to be smooth but rough with
The sand gravelled into it from the beach
The Galon D'or - overlapping waves tumble down onto
                                    the sun bleached
Sand people lay on.

Carolyn Sullivan (15)
Cardiff High School

70 Miles

70 miles is such a far-off place
I wonder what I'll find along the way
Perhaps a rose that blossoms in the face
Of desperate fragile dangers of the day
Or icy fire that burns a breathless flame
And leaks its cast-off ashes to the snow
While laughing as if death is just a game
70 miles is a long way to go
I don't know what I'll find or what I'll do
I'd travel all those miles and more for you.

Anwen Hayward (14)
Cardiff High School

Broken Glass

My heart has broken into tiny smithereens,
Blood trickles around my body,
Being tempted to stop,
There's no longer a strong beat,
Just silence.

My heart was made of thin glass,
The slightest touch,
And it's smashed,
There is no way of perfectly mending,
A broken piece of glass.

Ellie Kilroy (15)
Cardiff High School

The Closed Door

I edge up the cold grey steps
The door waits
It waits to be opened
The marks on the door are caught in the corner of my eye
They are blackened by flames that are no longer alight
A gush of wind hits me and rustles the leaves
Of the elderly tree standing proud and tall,
Elevated beside me,
The road behind me travels as far as the eye can see,
My inner child comes out and reaches for the door,
But she hesitates for a moment and pulls back her hand,
She moves and disappears from sight as if the wind has
                                              carried her away,
Curiosity has been beaten,
And what lies behind that door must wait for another day.

Kate Sansom (16)
Cardiff High School

Touch The Blossoms

Touch the blossoms falling from the trees,
The soft petals caressing your fingers,
You would see copses of trees surrounding you,
The sun peeking through the clouds.

If I took you there,
You would see copses of trees surrounding you,
You would hear laughter and chatter
Touch the blossoms falling from the trees,
The soft petals caressing your fingers
You would hear laughter, chatter.

I want to stay!

If I took you there you would see canopies,
Of trees hanging above you.

I want to stay here forever!

If only I could describe this place in words
I grew up here in my childhood dream
So, touch the blossoms
And you will see.

Rhyanne El-Nazer (15)
Cardiff High School

Imagine A World. . .

Imagine a world which you live in alone. . .
No one to play with
No one to see
Adventuring around God's green Earth
Around icy mountains alone. . .
Over towering canyons alone. . .
Trekking the world alone
No one to meet, to know, to talk to
No one to entertain, argue with or care for

Imagine a world in which nothing exists
A huge blank space unfilled, forgotten
No people, no cities, no towns, no animals
No planets, no stars, no galaxies, no outer space
No light, no colour, no heat, no anything
A vast mass of nothingness
To try to see this world would be impossible
Nothing, meaning nothing can live there
Nothing can enter, nothing can come out

Imagine a world where there was no sound
Nothing to hear forever
A wonderful, colourful, bright world
Muted. . .
People in the streets,
Walk up and down them
But as their mouths open and close
Nothing comes out
A complete silence that hangs over the world.

David Jiang (13)
Cardiff High School

The Chessboard

The pawns go in first
Two paces forward
Brothers against brothers
Fathers against their sons
Surely this isn't right
But it is not their decision to make
It is their leaders.

But when all is lost in come the bishops
With all their spiritual powers
But surely this isn't right
It is against their religion
But it is not their decision to make
It is their leaders!

The almighty leaders go in last.
The king is protected by the almighty queen.
But surely this isn't right
Shouldn't the king protect the queen?
But this isn't their decision to make
It is their leaders.

Sam Cooper (13)
Cardiff High School

Life

Destiny, believe, can't be predicted
It is only the way forward
The way to happiness and forgiveness
The way to guilt and despair
Sometimes it casts clouds of shadow
And sometimes showers of bloom
For destiny is mysterious.

The seasons, believe, are existence
The existence of mankind
For spring marks a brand new beginning
A beginning that will form
Like flowers flourishing in the garden
Summer leads us to growth, structure and wisdom
Like the trunk of a tree
Autumn comes, with the grown
Soon to become the dying
With the leaves falling off their branch of life
After that the cold winter comes
With the dark nights and the disappearance of life
Because of the white fluffy blanket, that covers all

Lives, believe, grow old and wither away
For it isn't our decision to depart
But it depends on us, the guardians
To expand and develop our future
To create a new beginning for others
As our life ends

Life is special for each and every one of us
We need to follow the path that lies ahead
We are all part of the world's existence
We are life.

Karen Borcenio Davies (13)
Cardiff High School

Untitled

Regal and refined is the tiger
Independent yet successful
Alas, their numbers declining all the same

During the blistering day, they lounge around
Soaking up the sizzling sun, enjoying life
Seeking to buy time, still it's rapidly running out

Though keeping a watchful eye out
For the shot aimed their way
Body tense, ready to make their gallant escape

From the poachers waiting to shoot
To exchange their striking, striped fur for coins and notes
Heartless, treacherous thieves selling stolen goods.

The tiger is an aristocrat
Tearing away to seize his victim, his last feast
For tomorrow his days may be over.

Sophie Baggott (13)
Cardiff High School

The Wood

The eerie green light peers through the upper canopy
Caused by the beautiful layer of leaves
The fresh smell of damp wood floats in my nostrils
This must be the nicest place on Earth.

The sun is starting to sink through the sky like a coin sinking in water
I must find a way out before darkness falls
But I am lost.
Darkness falls and the comforting glow of the eerie green light is gone
Branches stretch out to grab me and capture me
Deadly ivy winds its way round trees trying to suffocate them to death.

I start to run, I will do anything to get out of this horrible place
Thud!
I lie sprawled at the bottom of a tree after tripping over a thick root
The darkness surrounds me not giving me room to breath
As I get to my feet a sharp pain shoots up my leg
I'm stuck here for the night.

Oliver Jefferies (13)
Cardiff High School

This Boy I See

A heavy guitar pick, plastic to touch
Must have liked guitar very much

His mobile phone
Receiving a call, from 'unknown'

A movie stub, ripped down the middle
In his pocket, cared for little

A note, a 50p coin and a pound
As he walked, he made a jingly sound

A photo of a black dog
In the background a misty fog

Three gold keys on a rugby key ring
The serrated edges in the sun gleaming

An elastic band,
Stretching around

A World Cup ticket
Bending and curling in, a hint of blood splattered on it

This is all we found in his jeans
He had drowned, it seems.

Michael Coliandris (13)
Cardiff High School

Why?

What happened?
How?
When?
Where?
Why?

Shall I answer?
Shall I not?
Why are these people asking?
Do they have the right?
Can I even tell?

What next?
Why this?
Can I help?
Shall I go away?
Why?

Why do they bother?
Can't they go away?
Don't they realise I need some time just to be on my own?
Why now do they notice?
How do they know?

What happened?
How come?
Are you alright?
Are you sure?
Absolutely sure?

How do I begin?
What should I say?
Why are they here?
They are all around me,
But why?

Livia Frankish (13)
Cardiff High School

What If . . . ?

You stupid fat cow, leave us alone
Salty tears run down my cheek as they start to moan

Nobody likes you, cos you think you're all it
They're right, with this crowd I just don't fit.

The bell chimes, school comes to an end
I sprint like lightning through the gates and around the bend.

I only blame myself, I should be clever not stupid
I should be human not a cow,
All my thoughts are starting to flow now.

I've kept it all in for so long,
Yet I cannot find the strength to be strong.

I need some help what should I do?

A glint in the room gets my attention
A razor-sharp blade, perfect for releasing tension

I grab the blade and dig it in
Deeper it goes into my skin.

Weaker and weaker, my energy's gone
Falling to the floor, it takes too long

Now lying in my crimson pool of blood I have one last thought,

What if . . . ?

Tanya Owen (13)
Cardiff High School

About This Person

An iPod with a rubber blue case,
A picture of his mother's face.

His mobile phone screen,
Saying 'ring home'.

One trainer tied, one trainer not
His body has begun to rot.

Mud scattered all over the place,
Blood smeared all over his face.

A rucksack, lying on his back
The left strap seems to have snapped

His trousers torn, his T-shirt ripped
Of his money, he has been stripped.

In his pocket, a sandwich lies
Covered over, but swarmed in flies.

The body's front two teeth, missing from the gum,
On his forehead, a bullet wound from a gun.

Rhys Polley (13)
Cardiff High School

A God's Eye View Of The World

A beautiful world, tainted
By a blackened nightmare
Reality is a dream
In which there is no escape

Screams of pain crawl
Across the desolate charcoal sky
The sea which was once alive with peace
Now churns and crashes with agony
Against the crooked cliffside

The trees which held their arms up high
Now clasp the forest ground
In desperate attempt to keep their land

In this world, night prevails
But occasionally light breaks through
Erasing the smile which plays at its lips

It defines the trust we have in each other
It melts away the bitterness against us
We see the hope
We feel the freedom
Soon the tainted image will either away
Leaving light to shine through our soul.

Sadia Zaman (14)
Cardiff High School

Self Harm

Warm crimson blood trickles onto the floor
As the blade digs deeper and my arm gets sore

'You're ugly,' they say, 'you're spotty and fat,'
But it's getting so hard to 'just ignore' that

As I look in the mirror, gently resting on my wall
I can see I'm wide and not that tall

And as my tears make puddles of salt on the floor
I pack all my belongings and head for the door

I'm lonely and isolated, depressive and sad
My heart thumping quickly, my mind going mad

Blood pours from great gashes, I fall on my knees
Crying great rivers that turn into seas.

My life is messed up
I'm shaking with fear

I know I need help
Please somebody hear

I detest myself, I hate my life
And that's why I'm turning to the knife!

Lizzie Milne (13)
Cardiff High School

Being Bullied

The clenched, stiff fist was like a boulder crashing into my stomach
Pain wrapped round my vulnerable body squeezing tighter and tighter
This was the sequence of life
A leather boot was an arrow piercing my bruised and battered skin
Today I was lucky, tomorrow would be worse

This time pain gripped harder, its claws digging into my
defenceless skin
I flinched as the vicious mouth of the pin tore my flesh apart
Mocking laughter entered my ear deafening and ripping my eardrums
Today I was lucky, tomorrow would be worse

Today pain devoured my muscles leaving only the scraps
A weighted stone shone in the sunlight only to land in my eye
Making me howl for help
Followed by a sweet jab, oozing out the grief steadily
like a ketchup bottle clogged up
Today I was lucky, tomorrow would be worse.

Bilal Hussein (13)
Cardiff High School

Love And Hate

As I walk through the valley of demented dreams
I hold onto my head, and fall apart at the seams
I fall into my mind, my own universe
Taken away from the scene in my own little hearse
In my mind everything seems so hectic
Everyone around me is ever so sceptic
About my beliefs and self hatred fuelled ideas
Condemned a fake by my stupid, hating peers
In the tunnels of hope I'm surrounded by light,
Until I wade unto the darkness and get a fright,
That my whole mind is a maze full of walls,
That enclose on me until I begin to fall
Away from this insanity of reality
And into a world of a bad gals profanity
And into a universe of godforsaken denial
My thoughts of love and hate, stacked in a huge pile
Then as I wake up and think of my life,
To make it better is now my goal to strive,
Then I take a look in the mirror and realise its only me,
And the answer to happiness comes, you are the key!

Ethan Tann-Wood (14)
Cardiff High School

Forgiveness

On that fateful day
He came with a gun and a plan
He walked into their sanctuary, perished on the floor they lay
His plan had succeeded and the next noise heard was a bang.

The community came and saw what he had done
But they did not judge him, not a single one
They did not see him as a villain or a murderer
They saw a troubled man with a mental illness
Drowned in a pool of his own blood

The Amish came and they forgave him for his sins
For this is what they believe in.

Forgiveness.

Claudia Gallo (13)
Cardiff High School

My Magic Box

(Inspired by 'Magic Box' by Kit Wright)

In my box, my magic box
I will place the world's treasures
Treasures of great, treasures of power
I will place the world's greatest treasures

I will put in my box,
The sand and the sea,
The blood-red horizon,
And the settling golden sun.

Secondly, I will put it in my box
The silver tears of the moon,
The silver glimmer of the stars,
And the veil of the night sky.

Thirdly, I will put in my box,
The breath of an autumn's air,
The silk in a hazelnut,
And the gem of the forest.

My box is fashioned from,
The waves of the Caribbean,
The frost of the north,
And the soul of the Earth,
My box is bound through friendship, love and courage
Though I may be gone, my box lives on
Forever and ever.

Ben Guan (13)
Cardiff High School

The Volcano

The silence echoes through the crisp morning air,
No one is prepared for what will happen next.

Suddenly, a loud rumbling awakens the sleeping scenery
Bang! A huge explosion, smoke pierces the air

Lava spewing out, like a fountain of fire
People scream and run, but they cannot escape.

The molten lava engulfs everything in its path,
A thick woollen blanket covering the whole land.

And when there is nothing left for it to destroy,
The world is quiet again. Until the next time.

Sally Ivens (13)
Cardiff High School

A Love Spell . . .

Throw in some rainbows and a few happy smiles,
A teaspoon of laughter to last for miles.

1 gram of loyalty, another of trust,
A valentine's chocolate with a lovely hard crust.

The touch of a baby, some secret vows,
A lot of kind talk, no room for rows.

The first ever oak tree, the feather of a dove
Mix it all together and you've got love!

Angela Thomas (14)
Cardiff High School

Love

A sprinkle of sugar
A dash of hearts
A touch of friendship
So that they never fall apart
A handful of passion
Stir in hugs and kisses
Make sure you put in your wishes
A piece of a white wedding dress
The feather of a white turtle dove
These are the things that make love.

Samyukta Shetty (14)
Cardiff High School

Love

Love is like being as light as a feather
Love is being apart but still together

Love is like no one can touch you
Love is when you saw him and knew

Love is when you only see him
Love is happy and never grim

Love is when you know he's not perfect
Love is having a different effect

Love is thinking about him day and night
Love is knowing it will all be alright

Love is seeing him how no one else does
Love is love just because.

Lucy Oyler (14)
Cardiff High School

The Sound Of Silence

Schools in America are different to ours
Schools in Pennsylvania are different worldwide
Especially on this day of disturbance
There was a smell of rotting flesh,
Not a flattering fragrance,
The atmosphere was tense as an awkward silence struck,
There the culprit was, standing there before us
The tube of doom now loaded,
All children began to plea, 'What will we have done wrong?
Please forgive me.'
The answer to this question was now too late,
It was left for police to find out and the parents to wait
The culprit was however mentally ill,
But why sweet, innocent school girls the ones to be killed?
The answer for this gunshot wasn't a pill
And how we now wish a dove could fly by,
For peace to be blessed as the parents cry,
The death of the school girls began to be gross,
But will a gift of forgiveness,
Compare to the parents tragic loss?

Ellis Hiles (14)
Cardiff High School

Nothing But You

After I saw you, I noticed that never have I seen anything
As beautiful as you
Your beauty always reminds me of the glow of the new full moon
I'm so happy that you happened to come into my life
With you I've been able to fight some of life's strife

I have never ever seen such perfect eyes
Every time I look into them its like looking in the sunrise
Since I love your smile, all I like to do is make you laugh
Even we go our separate ways, your smile will always last
In my heart lies your face, I always think of you
You brighten up my day, in your special way.

Never before have I seen anybody as perfect as you
I've even experienced new feelings that are all so new
It never occurred, to me the first time I saw your face
I would fall so deep in love
I always think about all the crazy things you do
Because now and until the end of time, I will always love you.

Yousuf Nadeem (14)
Cardiff High School

Darkness Falls

Time is up,
The day's gone,
You had your chance,
And threw it away.

Twilight is here,
Livid orange and reds
Light up the sky,
Stillness haunts the air.

No animals stir,
Only stillness crows this cocoon,
Tears stream down your face,
As you watch darkness take over.

Silhouettes of the trees,
Sway in the breeze,
How could something so burning,
Ruin this magical scene?

Blazing fires erupt around you,
Colours so bright,
Trancing you,
Until you're gone.

You don't remember,
Once more it's taking over,
The sky is turning,
Darkness falls.

Lucy Burrows (14)
Cardiff High School

Global Warming

The world is getting hotter,
But no one seems to care.
The seasons are all better,
Snow and ice we don't get our share!

Icicles in the summer
Hurricanes in spring,
Clothes we need to order
Bathers or woolly things?

Greenhouse effect or natural?
It does not really mind,
We have to deal with actual
And try to save mankind.

Coal in the boiler,
Kerosene in planes,
Heating up the toiler,
And wasting down the drains.

The oceans will not get deeper,
Archimedes tells us that,
But an earlier date with the Reaper,
Unless we can stop the tat.

Buy another planet?
Go to outer space?
Boy, it's getting harder
To save the human race.

Hang on it's 6 o'clock
Nearly time for tea!
I'll go and watch the television
Before saving history.

David Evans (14)
Cardiff High School

The Somme Theatre

Here we are standing now
Wishing you to applaud us as we take our final bow
We are the professionals
The masters of the art
Yet even we can get stage fright
Standing still as statues while the director dictates each
character's face.

Now the moment you've all been waiting for
Our shows most admired scene
We run onto the treacherous stage
And a thousand instruments begin to play
The musicians each playing their dreaded song
As we fight the battle of the Somme
Yet we still run
To the sound of the guns.

Alas that was our grand finale
And the end of the show
Once again we have lost the stage fight
And now fresh innocent blood flows
So please applaud, cheer and jeer
Because we are bloody kings, on our tainted thrones.

Rhys Wilkinson (14)
Cardiff High School

Goal!

As you're running with the ball at your feet
You get more confident every time you pass someone with ease,
What emotion you'll experience you'll never know,
But you could experience it all in one go.

There will be highs, there will be lows
There'll be moments you triumph, there will be moments you won't
Suddenly you'll be on top of the world but back down to earth
Quicker than you know
Everyone will be on your side one moment and then you'll be alone.

When you're on top of your game you can't be stopped
You don't want to think about the face of a clock
You feel you can go forever and never tire,
There's a burning desire within you and you're only stoking up the fire.

Teammates will always will you on until you finish
When there's a 50-50 ball you've got to win it
When you play you play knowing football is known as
'the beautiful game'.
And when you win it tastes sweet, like a sugar cane.

It can be a messy experience, like the eruption of lava
Whether you're serious or having a laugh it is never short of drama,
You will relish every kick and every touch,
When you're doing well you get the adrenaline rush.

There will be times when anger crosses the mind
There will be a moment when someone oversteps the line,
Any frustration will quickly be sorted,
Any possible acts of violence will be thwarted.

It's called the beautiful game because it brings difficult people together
Friendships might be made which last forever
During the game there's one great moment on the whole,
The ball hitting the net and everyone shouting goal!

An-noor Rahman (14)
Cardiff High School

An Ideal World

Children travelling miles each day just to drink
They could be at school, with friends, with loved ones
Selfish people look upon them,
They do nothing to try to help,
They see school as a chore,
While there are those who dream of education.

Starvation and death,
Two powerful words that are ignored,
Money spent on useless activities
Food wasted like there's enough in the world

Coppers and silvers spent on useless items
Beneficial to only yourself
Many starving, homeless, ill
Do you know how much you kill?

Walking past a man in a box,
Without giving a second glance,
To avoid giving some charity
Outcasts in our society.

Trying to fix other problems when plagued by ones of your own
Education, healthcare, crime
Only to list a few.

Plastic, knives, needles and fumes,
Thousands of pounds,
Can you guess?
Plastic surgery
Money spent on ruining what God gave you,
Not happy or just no confidence in life?

What an ideal world.

William Tai (14)
Cardiff High School

The Sound Of Silence

Schools in America are different to ours
From this school, screams came, came from the towers

Schools and children are different worldwide
But in this Amish school the children died

The small innocent children were asking this man
Please, please don't make that fateful bang!

Why, why, why was it them?
The madman said nothing, nothing again

The awful silence rang through the hall
The madman still said nothing, standing so tall

The parents were still waiting, was it all too late
Were the little girls to come to their fate?

The girls lay quiet, so quiet, so cold
The blood on the floor was red and bold

The girls' luck had all gone
But from the hearts of their families
Only love had shone

Forgiveness, in this case was the only key
And in this small town, they planted a tree

A tree that would stand so tall
And a tree that would stand up, up for them all.

Verity Jeffreys (14)
Cardiff High School

Wales

The Welsh dragon standing so tall
When I see it, I look so small
I'm proud to be born in Wales
A land full of hills and dales

Castle towers reach to the sky
Were they conquered we can but try
Such a lovely little place
Where you're bound to see friendly face

My grandfathers worked down the mine
From the age of twelve to the time
They dragged the coal to the top
Until the foreman he did cry stop

The port bells are not ringing
They haven't worked since the beginning
The goods are coming in
There's bound to be a din

Snowdon, standing up very high
Reaching much further than the sky
All rocky and rough
This place looks tough

I am proud to be born in Wales
And listen to my family's tales
The stories that are told -
Of my ancestors of old.

Aneira Hayward (14)
Cardiff High School

Don't Get Bullied

Day by day people poke fun
But they may take it differently
Day by day
Rumours spread, rumours spread
Made a joke of
Day by day
Verbal abuse
Shouting, shouting
For all the world to hear
People laughing, laughing
Think of how the person feels
Day by day
Think of the person
A fire building up inside
Building and building up
But after a while
The fire will explode
And they will fight back
Maybe in violence or maybe
In speaking to someone
Day by day
To let it all be sorted
Day by day.

Steven Tarrant (14)
Cardiff High School

Freezing Point

A gush of icy, crisp air passed the figure of an unconscious man
nearing his death
Fear once grew though the man's solemnest
Frozen horror rose a paradise of tightly threaded woe. It was his
freezing point

Hope had gone when the dogs fled away, along with best mate Dave
Icy crystals formed an invisible layer
The once conqueror was a folding vision of power once man's prize
I told him to stop but he just said no
His visions haunted by a blood-covered beast coming towards him in
his sleep
Yep, this was his freezing point

The wounds on his back just wouldn't heal and left a hollow scab
running through his veins
The beast had come to haunt his fears and closely come to finish
the job
Yes this is the freezing point

The rescue team finally punched through, the essence of death
covered in ice
The body frozen to the floor was a sign of failed attempts past and
future and for evermore
And this was his freezing point.

Harry Greenway (13)
Cardiff High School

Freedom

(Sbwriel - Welsh word meaning 'rubbish')

Rolling around
The city
Free
Full of life
Energy
Flowing through
Like a shot of vodka
Hitting you from behind
Feet shaking
But
In a vibe sensation of life
As I jump
Jumping in the air
Higher than the sky
Over the box
Spinning and flipping
As if I'm flying like a pig
As I land
I know life's going to the norm
And will be back
To the same old sbwriel
And a feeling of lifeness leaves me.

Benjamin Crook (15)
Radyr Comprehensive School

Crocospi!

I wouldn't go near him if I were you
His deep blue eyes staring at you
Snap go his teeth when you stretch out your hand
Don't move a muscle
Don't even stand

His teeth are like knives, shiny and white
If you look at them closely, you'll have a fright

Crocospi's body is as sharp as a blade
The jewels on the edge look neatly made
His arms are so sharp, spiky like a hedgehog
With green slimy skin
The same as a bullfrog

Last is his legs
The spidery type
The ones that come crawling in your bed every night

He lives in a swamp
With trees all around
There's green muddy slime
All over the ground.

Jessica Watkins (11)
Radyr Comprehensive School

Anger

I have hair like fire
And a screaming face
I have a knife as an arm
And a gun as a leg
I have a bomb as a foot
And a broken plate as a body

I live in a war field
And smell like smoke
I make everyone angry
From Paris to Africa
I am constantly screaming
Wherever I go.

Rebecca Marshall (12)
Radyr Comprehensive School

The Volcano's Head

Just like the person's head
The volcano sleeps as if in bed
The large round boulders
Just like the person's shoulders
The volcano goes *kaboom!*
Creating the person's tomb
The volcano erupts, the spot bursts
The lava trickles down first
The large crater at the top in the skies
Looks like the person's eyes
The volcano leaves no one alive that day
The person turns and walks away.

Cameron MacDonald (13)
Radyr Comprehensive School

School

A brand new day is exploding
Red and black gushing through like lava
Acidic teachers guarding the corridors
The odd sparkly child reading a book
The fiery bullies pushing past
The deep classrooms with different types of children
Like soft and hard rock
Steam gushing out teacher's head in frustration as they teach
Pencils flying everywhere like ash
As the bell rings the pupils leave like fast flowing lava.

Emily Bright (13)
Radyr Comprehensive School

A Busy Street

A busy street is like a volcano
Smoke coming from the cars
People are flowing down the street
Cones everywhere
Pavement cracked
Shops blasting with people
Stones flying up from the road
Lights turn red
Everything stops
Lights turn green
Everything goes again
Back to normal.

Alex Coombes (13)
Radyr Comprehensive School

The Hectic Volcano

A person's head is like a volcano,
Bright red lava builds up in him,
He gets angry and begins to erupt
Green rivers come out of his nose
Steam bursts out of his ears
His cheeks become flame-red
He gets into a fight and gets hit
Red lava starts to come out of his nose

A teacher comes and the 'volcano' cools down.

Minh-Tri Lam (13)
Radyr Comprehensive School

Supermarket Volcano!

The supermarket is like a volcano;
The sound of babies are deafening
And the smell of the fish section is unpleasant
It erupts your nose

The trolleys are like massive trucks
Carrying massive rocks
The frozen food is freezing
Contributing to a volcano

The car park is like an acid sea
Cars on every island, nowhere to park
The beeping of the checkout makes
You feel it will explode!

Pritesh Varsani (13)
Radyr Comprehensive School

The Deadly School

Everyone running through the corridors like a fast flowing river
People smell from running like the fishy ocean smell on a wet day
Teachers are lifeless and dumb like a goldfish
The school's water supply seems like its shark-infested from the
fishy smell
School is just a big tank with us the little fish inside!

Vaughan Kenward (13)
Radyr Comprehensive School

Stadium

The magma building up as the fans fill up the stadium
The fans are ready to explode
When the players come out
The whole place is rumbling
As the players kick the round the ball
Gerrard shoots from far out
The ball goes in
Everyone jumps
The 90 minutes are up
The explosion has stopped
The skies are silent once again.

Jack Shellard (13)
Radyr Comprehensive School

Dallmonbee

Hello, my name is Dallmonbee
I hope you're having a good day
Because I'm about to make it
The *worst* day of your life
With my head so red
And spikes on my neck
And a Loch Ness grin and evil eyes

I am taller than mountains
I eat trees as a snack
But my bee-like body
With my sting so sharp
And wings so large
Gives off an aroma of honey
And the horrible *bzzzzz* of a wasp

But the very, very worst part has to be
The Dalek structure
And I elevate upstairs so you'd better watch out
As I live in the mountains
And I live in the woods
Exterminbzzzgrrr!

Laura Green (11)
Radyr Comprehensive School

Drunaphant

It prowls and growls
But thumps heavy
On the dusty desert ground
Flight takes time
But it doesn't get far
And ends up committing a crime

As it squishes animals
Such as spiders
Up high watching
Swishing and swooping is a glider
Back up in the air
Flying high with a lot of care
Eating pizza and drinking Coke
The only thing it hates is a cigarette
With some smoke

The desert hot and shadows glare
The sun is beating down
And the heat is a scare
For such creatures as a Drunaphant
This is not a problem
As it's a cross between a dragon, rabbit and an elephant.

Hannah Dykes (11)
Radyr Comprehensive School

The Snwarsander

In the deepest and darkest of mountain top caves
Lives the Snwarsarder
You should be afraid!
The monster has talons like sharp shiny knives
It's legs are like spiders
It's arms are like bears
Covered in long, dark brown hairs
It smells like the acrid smoke from a gun
Its tail's like a needle, pointy and sharp
The body's a wasp, yellow and black
Its head is a snake's head
A long, pointy tongue
If you listen in the dead of the night
A 'bbbzzzsss grr!' will give you a fright!

Sophie Shenton (11)
Radyr Comprehensive School

Robodragoder

You'll find him in an old, deserted church
Surrounded by an overgrown forest of grass and weeds
All mangled and twisted together
The weather there is stormy and dark
He's never seen the sun in his whole life
Robodragoder's head is a vast, silver square
Bearing two black, beady eyes
A white button nose and a blood-red mouth
His eyebrows are always pointing downwards and
His bright orange hair bursts out of his metal scalp
Robodragoder's neck is like a snake's
It squirms and writhes
Rocking his head from side to side
His monster's body is enormous and hairy
It sits on top of eight, windy legs
That are used for reaching out and snatching
People from their graves
Robodragoder's arms tower above him
They are green, red and scaly
Wings
Huge, skyscraper wings
Spanners are his hands
They snap at people and scare them away
Robodragoder smells of mouldy, green, manky cheese as well as
Stinky feet, rotten eggs *and* gone-off fish!
His breath stinks of garlic
Robodragoder hates people and is always alone.

Sophie Austin (11)
Radyr Comprehensive School

Snabeguife

Hello, my name is Snabeguife
My head is a ssnake
That will hiss at you with poison
My body iss a bee and
I will sting you all over
My hands and legs are knives and guns
I will torture you with them
And if none of that works
My smell of rotten eggs
Will get rid of you.

Briony Powell (12)
Radyr Comprehensive School

Freddy The Monster

His name is Freddy
He's full of hate
His hair is fire
And he won't be your mate

He has red eyes
His habitat is brown
He has spiky teeth
And he always has a frown

He has snakes for arms and
Has no real charms
A body of a shark's fin
And is full of sin

Seaweed for legs
Chainsaws for feet
Fingers of pegs and
Toes of wheat

So beware of Freddy
Because he will eat you up
Don't go near him
Or your blood he will sup.

Emma Williams (12)
Radyr Comprehensive School

Back To School!

I just woke up this morning
Jumped slowly out of bed
Brushed my teeth and washed my face
And gosh was my face red!

My mum said, 'Time for school love.'
I said, 'OK, OK!'
Thought, *where is my uniform?*
'Come on, you're gonna be late!'

On my way to school, I passed lots of trees
Then I heard a river, *splash*
I ran over just to see

It looked like a big rat
It smelt like really strong acid
I said, 'Hey that stinks!'
So I carried on and passed it.

I got to school
But it was too quiet
The ground erupted
On no, it's a riot!

When I got home I was dull and tired
Just found out my dad got fired!

Sophia Homayoonfar (13)
Radyr Comprehensive School

Christmas

Christmas
Snow is falling
Happy faces everywhere

Christmas
Big green trees up
Twinkly lights shining

Christmas
Presents being wrapped by the dozen
Children getting excited

Christmas
Minced pies being put out
Reindeer enjoying their carrots

Christmas
It goes too fast
I want it to last
But I'll just have to wait until next year.

Lydia Le Saux (13)
Radyr Comprehensive School

Imaginary Journey

Travelling on my watermelon
To an aweseome land
Over in the distance
I can see the golden sand

Balloons up in the air
Carrying my surfboard
With all this help
I feel like a lord

As I get nearer
I can see a sparkly diamond ring
People playing volleyball
And peacefully sunbathing

Oh no! What's that?
Down beneath me is a shark,
But to make me laugh,
I see Cartman from South Park

So many 'hot' surfers
Maybe I'll get a wink
Wow, that looks nice
The dude with the big cocktail drink

Suddenly something appeared
Just randomly out of the blue
It's a very large mouth
Asking questions like 'who are you?'

I think I'm dreaming
Someone pinch me now
Where did this mouth come from?
Why's it here, and how?

Laura Burford (13)
Radyr Comprehensive School

Hole In The Wall

It started at home, not a long time ago
I felt really bored, it was too hot to snow
I felt like an adventure, I got into my ship
I stepped on the throttle, I gripped the gear stick
Off I went, into a journey through time
I landed pretty soon, into a pool of green slime
I was sinking, oh dear, this couldn't be the right place
I flew and landed, I saw a ball with a smug face,
'Greetings', they said, 'you're just in time for lunch.'
They grabbed hold of me as I tricked and punched
I shouted at them, 'What do you want with me?'
They replied, 'Nothing much, you just look tasty.'
They grabbed me and shoved me into a large pot
It was full of water, it was really hot
I tipped the pot over and ran for my soul
They had built a big wall, I looked for a hole
There was no escape and the things were getting near
So I wished that my ship would magically appear
I talked for my ship and if came straight away
I got in and shouted, 'Have a nice day.'
The wall was no match to the power of my ship
I pushed the power button with my fingertips
I had survived the planet that remains unknown
And lucky for me I arrived safely home.

Thomas Spiteri (12)
Radyr Comprehensive School

The UFO

We're on a UFO
We are
Travelling in space
We've met loads of new friends
Like the aliens in this place
The sun and stars glistening and blinding me
But all you can see is mist in front
We don't know where we're going
Who cares we're in space
There could be a monster, there could be a sea
There could be a black hole
But it's only a maybe.

Cherie Roberts (12)
Radyr Comprehensive School

Yankee 911

Yankee 911 was called
We jumped aboard to save the world
And entered the cloudy night sky
The search light on
As we gazed around
And came upon a flying cloud
Upon that flying cloud I saw
An amazing flying fairy world
A beautiful castle with flowers to
Decorate the midnight sky
As the castle disappeared
We drove through the space
Where it had appeared
And went to tell people
The amazing things that we'd seen.

Laura Anderton (13)
Radyr Comprehensive School

Razor

I am Razor, I will cut you to a million pieces
I was born in a volcano
Which blew lava out and made me.
Anyone who wants to mess with me
I will punch them power level three.
My snake hair will spray you with venom
And then I will eat you at my lair.
My tattooed weapons will become real
And then I will make you my meal.

Michael Flowers (12)
Radyr Comprehensive School

Tommyfang Hornclaw

He attacks quietly the homes at night
He never leaves a trace
He tears the flesh off the bone
And leaves only the face

He fires at his victims and cannot miss
He collects the bullet shells
He feeds his mother and younger sis
With flesh and bladder that smells

They live under villages
Cities, hamlets and towns
They move from home to home
With frightful roaring sounds

But Tommyfang hunts the prey
He collects them alive
When Tommyfang gets violent
No one can survive!

Marc Davies (13)
Radyr Comprehensive School

My Big Fat Bully Is

A way in a cave in the bubbly bath of lava
N ever washes and makes me feel nauseous
G nawing away at the flesh and bones of humans, bears and hares
R ough, rugged and round, is the cave in the ground, where he
                                    roams around and around
Y ellow wings flying around.

Adam Pincombe (12)
Radyr Comprehensive School

My Suntreeflower

My head is a big circle
It looks like the sun
I'm always glad to see you
I'll smile at anyone

My one arm is a flower
And the other is a Christmas tree
My legs are made of candy canes
As you can probably see

I live up in Heaven
Where there are lots of treats
My belly is a birthday cake
It would taste rather sweet.

Oliver Haines (12)
Radyr Comprehensive School

Winalot

I always have to finish first
I really love to win
I don't rest until I'm done
I have a power within

My arms are broken finish lines
First place flashes in my eyes
I'm placed upon a podium
My hope fills the skies

I live on a race track
Getting faster every day
When I know I'm gonna win
Is the reason I'll play

My Olympic circle body
May look quite divine
They might make me feel empty
But winning makes me fine.

Sarah Carroll (12)
Radyr Comprehensive School

The Pet I've Always Wanted

My pet's amazing
He's smaller than a cat
He always lies down on his back
And loves a good old pat

My pet's fantastic
And now I've called it Ted
But he is a bit lumpy
I wouldn't hug him in bed

My pet's marvellous
We always go on walks
We go all the way through the woods
But he doesn't exactly talk

My pet's magnificent
Even though he is quite thick
That's because good old pet
Is nothing more than a brick.

Luke Gilbert (12)
Radyr Comprehensive School

Mystery Murderer

Most of you hate me
Some of you love me
I rip people's lives apart
I bring people in to me to make me bigger
I kill millions
But I don't care
I bring people from miles away
There has only been two occasions where I've killed millions
Some you run far, far away
I am like no other
You try to win me
You can run, but you can't hide I will get you eventually
I am not a disease
But I spread all across the world
I am not a drug
But people can still get high on me
I am the mystery murderer
My name
War.

Perry Rowlands (12)
Radyr Comprehensive School

When You Love Someone

When you're in love
You know how it's meant to feel
You get so many butterflies
That make it all so real

When you tell them you love them
It's not just something to say
When you say that you care
It's not just for the day

We both know the meaning of love
And why it reaches our heart
How forever is forever
And we'll never part

Because love is like
The clouds in the sky
Love can't be love
Without the 'you' and the 'I'

It takes two people to make love
Two halves to make a whole
Love is tender love
From the bottom of your soul.

Roseanne Payne (14)
Radyr Comprehensive School

Echo

The word slips from my mouth
Why?
It starts running and playing
Like a kitten
It starts bouncing
Off the walls

It gets carried
Away
By the wind
Until I cannot hear it
Anymore

But I know it will keep
Travelling on
Through waterfalls
Through walls
Until one day, maybe
Somebody will find my little 'why'?
And answer it
For me.

Kate Anderson (12)
Ysgol Gyfun Gymraeg Plasmawr

Away With Words

I love my mummy so very much
And for her I'm going to be brave
Because she's taking me down to the cemetery
To visit Daddy's grave

I love my daddy so very much
He died in the 9/11
He was the best daddy in the world
And I know he's gone to Heaven

Tears run down my face
Mum says it's OK to cry
But the worst thing I can think of
Is that I never said goodbye

There are no words to describe how I'm feeling
So I will not even try
The only word that will be heard from me is
Oh why, oh why, oh why?

Ffion Wright (13)
Ysgol Gyfun Gymraeg Plasmawr

Away With Words

What are words?
Pointless sounds to explain your opinions
When people can't be *bothered* taking action
They make promises that are *never* kept

They say that they have a way with words
But I say *away* with words
Music explaining topics
A way to show *your opinion* on life

Gestures a *true* way to show your feelings
Of *love* or *hate* and blame to the world
And you remember all those times
The times that *you yourself* have used words

To explain *your* feelings
To explain your view and opinions
To make promises that have *never* been kept
And you realise that you are no different *to them*

Words are *your life*
You *only* way to contact the world
To get your opinion across
There is *no way* to banish them.

Cerys Lane (12)
Ysgol Gyfun Gymraeg Plasmawr

The Zoo

As I walked into the zoo
I could hear the pitter-patter of the rain
Falling heavily
Against the hard terrain

The roar of the lion
As it got wet
And the sound of the monkeys
Beginning to fret

The birds stopped tweeting
Because the sky was grey
A rustling of the leaves
And then they flew away

The pumping of the heart
Was all that I could hear
The animals were waiting
For the sun to appear

Suddenly - *whoosh* a gust of wind
The clouds began to fade
Then with a cheer of triumph
The animals' day had been made.

Anders Roblin (13)
Ysgol Gyfun Gymraeg Plasmawr

A Way With Words

A guy in school with a way with words,
A charm like you wouldn't believe;
Says absolutely anything,
And you blush so red, you grieve!

He asks, 'What's wrong?' but you really can't say,
His comments just swept you away;
You look uptight; well he looks just fine,
And you wonder why you came in today.

It starts to rain, oh lovely - just great!
Now I'm blushing and wet;
My hair goes all curly and my feet go damp,
A morning I know I'll regret!

Why so charming? - This guy I mean,
And why's my hair all curls?
I guess it's my stupid luck,
That this guy has a way with words.

Indeg Williams (12)
Ysgol Gyfun Gymraeg Plasmawr

Away With Words

How would we celebrate
And chatter and play
When we could not express our feelings
To those that we spend the day
In their delightful company
We should laugh most joyfully
But instead we are captured
Without a reason to live
All mouths are glued together
This is not how we should live
Captured in quietness
When one of our gifts
Is slaughtered and killed
And shattered and ripped
Beauty divine
Though captured with the eye
Can only be told
In words alone
And as words are added
So is magic and song
Which you can control
Where nothing goes wrong
Words are taken for granted
But without them
You see
The world would be lost
And so would we.

Anna Williams (13)
Ysgol Gyfun Gymraeg Plasmawr

Away With Words

There's my brother
Sitting on a plane

Plain white bread
Made with different flours

Flowers on the table
Looking very dear

Deer wandering everywhere
Over there and over here

Hear the whooshing sound
Made by the creeping sea

See my brother
Jumping over the tide

Tied around a wooden
Long and thin plank

Plankton in the sea
To feed all the whales

Wales the greatest
In the see

Mutations are hard!
Huh!

Angharad Rosser (12)
Ysgol Gyfun Gymraeg Plasmawr

Away With Words

When I'm reading
I'm not on my bed
I'm in a different world

A magical world where
I don't have to worry
About anything

I'm in an impossible place
Where unthinkable things happen
Where unthinkable people live

When I'm reading
My imagination
Lets anything and anyone come to life

When I'm reading
I'm not on my bed
I'm in a different world.

Caio Redknap (12)
Ysgol Gyfun Gymraeg Plasmawr

The Beach

The golden sand
Rushing through my hand
The waves in rage
Like animals inside a tiny cage
Like a raging bull
Then the rage stopped
So calm
So still
In the background there are many hills
And if you look hard you can see the seals
The sun is now leaving
Going with the wind.

Jordan Walcott (13)
Ysgol Gyfun Gymraeg Plasmawr

Santiago Bernabeau

The skills of David Beckham shock the defence
Like an earthquake
The fans cheering the players on
The smell of the hot dog makes your nose burst

The goals are brilliant but the set plays
Are the heart of the game
The drums beating like a bomb
Going off in World War I

The fans are roaring
Like a lion roaring in his pride
Then the goal of lightning went in
The net rippled, the fans thunder their applause.

Louis Uncles (13)
Ysgol Gyfun Gymraeg Plasmawr

Like A Dream

The golden sand
I stare at the sea
I thought I was dreaming
But I was here
Ibiza
The sun glaring
Pressing on my skin
As I stare at the sea
The sand between my toes
Children all around me
Laughing and playing
I think back to school
And giggle to myself
I think of my classmates
Doing their work
And I am here, enjoying
I'm here for a week
I wish I was here
For life.

Taylor Brady (13)
Ysgol Gyfun Gymraeg Plasmawr

Rugby Stadium

The green muddy grass
And the slippery slidy floor
The ball getting kicked
Like a bullet
Bang! Tackle!
Players go down
Players getting angry
And getting swung around
The crowd going wild
The happiness for a while
The tasty sparkling hot dogs
Greasy and very hot
Half the crowd is laughing
Half the crowd is crying
Half the crowd is living
And the other half is dying.

Matthew Lewis (13)
Ysgol Gyfun Gymraeg Plasmawr

Old Trafford

At the stadium,
With the fans warm,
The black air filled the sky,
And the noise at its loudest.

Hot dogs sizzle, whistle blows
Chocolate-covered hands,
Thirst-quenching Coke
The players like mice,
Run across the floor,
People chanting,
Screaming, laughing
Like fairies filled with joy,
As the referee looked at his watch,
To blow for full-time,
Rooney scores,
Hooray! Hooray!
Cheerio, cheerio, cheerio,
As the fans leave the stadium chanting,
The stadium goes dark.

Daniel Khan (14)
Ysgol Gyfun Gymraeg Plasmawr

Away With Words

A river of words winding through the lonely forest,
A brain is on the riverbank,
Fishing for a brilliant word to impress his boss,
He's caught the word it's rank, he smiles

Your mind is a dictionary of you
It's like a computer searching for a word,
It might make you a superstar saying something impressive,
Or you could become an enemy with a single story.

Personality, another thing that words affect
You can be posh by using large unheard of words
Or a chav by using short slang words like 'innit'
Or a correcter by knowing all that's right.

Words can place you on the map,
'Arai but' places you up in the Welsh valleys,
'Caaardiff' you come from Ely or Danescourt,
Or a very strong Welsh accent puts you in Bangor or the Bala.

Tomos Innes (13)
Ysgol Gyfun Gymraeg Plasmawr

The Prom

Here we are, the night of the year
Beautifully dressed students
Together for the last time
The music, the laughter
The drinking and the dancing
It's all so amazing,
Life-changing experience,
Boys and girls change to women and men
We all say goodbye
As this is the last night together
'I'll miss you all' everybody cries
For this is the moment the whole night dies.

Rachel Payne (13)
Ysgol Gyfun Gymraeg Plasmawr

Stadium

In the big stadium
I can see loads of fans
Screaming, jumping and kicking
The managers are sitting and concentrating
You can see loads of rubbish by the food bar
It smells of
Deodorant pumping through the air
Smoke from those
Who are nervous
You can see the managers
Jumping up and down like yo-yos
Because they are excited or angry
The players are sweating buckets of water
Because they are working hard
The players are charging down the field
Like a cheetah running after the ball
Rooney shoots
Goal!
1-0 to Man U
The final whistle blows
The end of the game.

Luke Campbell (13)
Ysgol Gyfun Gymraeg Plasmawr

Long Day

The sun was like a ball of fire
Burning on my skin
The waves were rising
The children were swimming
The soft sand in between my toes
Ice cream melting in between my fingers
Dance, sing
Mums and dads shout
Sandwiches lying on the sand
Seagulls gushing down like the wind
The day comes to an end
The sun reflecting on the clear sea
After a long day comes to an end.

Hannah Crimmins (13)
Ysgol Gyfun Gymraeg Plasmawr

Nightclub

Disco decks spinning
Music blaring
People dancing
Drunk people prancing

Everyone talking
Some people walking
Lots of people jumping
While the music is bumping.

All the cups are filled
With beer that's chilled
Every light flashing
Most of the people bashing.

Saturday night.

Rhys William Thomas (13)
Ysgol Gyfun Gymraeg Plasmawr

Away With Words

I doze away into another world
And all of my friends appear into the dream
I am on a football pitch
Wearing the green and white stripes of the team

Playing football against Arsenal
Playing football in the Premiership
Was I dreaming?
I didn't think I was

Suddenly I had the ball
I passed it to Iewan and he passed it back
I nutmegged Toure and ran with the ball
I shot at the goal it curled into the goal.

Playing football against Arsenal,
Playing football in the Premiership,
Was I dreaming?
I didn't think I was,
Until I woke up.

Cai Galea (12)
Ysgol Gyfun Gymraeg Plasmawr

The Wishing Machine

'All right', says Miss, 'I want a description of a household appliance.'
So I imagine that . . .

I take my load to the wishing machine
And chuck my problems in it
Instead of 40 degree or 50
Decide a wish - so problematic

I type in my little wish
And set it on to spinning
Wait a while until it's done
And take it out, smiling

I peg it on the wishing line
Along with 'get homework done'
'Buy some Prada shoes'
And 'go for a run'.

It's dry! I run upstairs
And see . . .

'Oh for goodness sake,'
Groans the teacher
'She's away with words again.'

Branwen Parry (12)
Ysgol Gyfun Gymraeg Plasmawr

Away With Words

I'm taking my favourite words away
With me on holiday

Pickle
Furiously
Pyjamas
Crinkly
Chocolate

There's no room in my suitcase for

Supercalifragilisticexpialidocious

Which is a shame,
So I'll have to leave it at home.

When I get to Mallorca,
I'm going to play with my words on the beach,
And *furiously* eat *crinkly chocolate* with *pickle* in my *pyjamas*!

Nan Moore (12)
Ysgol Gyfun Gymraeg Plasmawr

Away With Words

In my suitcase, I keep all my words
Under my towels, I tuck my vowels
To the right of that, I put my consonants
Next to my pounds, I place my nouns
And my adverbs are folded neatly to the left
By my dressing gown, I wrap up my pronouns
Beside my herbs (it's a self-catering holiday) are my verbs,
Over that I squeeze in my proper nouns,
Now I've arrived at beautifu . . .
Oh darn it, I've forgotten my adjectives.

Geraint Ballinger (13)
Ysgol Gyfun Gymraeg Plasmawr

Away With Words

To the finder of these words
I'm sending a message to the world
Whoever may find this
Wherever you may be
Across oceans and seas
In far distant lands
On any different continent
Send on your own message
To the next finder
Will it ever come back to me?
To the beach where I am?
It's an international chain
From country to country to country
Different nationalities
How long will it float around
In the wide open waters?
And now, away with these words
Away into the white waves
Cork on the bottle
Into the thrashing sea.

Rhys Waring (12)
Ysgol Gyfun Gymraeg Plasmawr

Away With Words

Away with words to Neverland
Non-fiction books I cannot stand.
Peter Pan and Captain Hook
These are characters in my book.

Now I'm wandering Middle-Earth,
Running away from Sauron's curse.
Frodo, Sam and Pippin too
Nail-biting stuff will they get through?

Harry Potter and Ron Weasley
Flying the car I'm quite queasy.
Dumbledore is quite a bore
Slytherin and Gryffindor go to war.

Away with words I love to go,
Lots of tales I'd love to know.
Many stories I have read,
Tired now - off to bed.

Carwyn Huw (12)
Ysgol Gyfun Gymraeg Plasmawr

Away With Words

I am away with words
Writing what comes to my mind
Imagining the birds
Flying by the border line

I am away with words
Flying high over the sea
The warm breeze in my face
And dreams flying next to me

I am away with words
Dreaming wildly into space
The never ending stars
Looking for that earthly place

I am away with words
Staring from the dark black sky
Gazing far down below
At the life passing by.

Siwan Reynolds (13)
Ysgol Gyfun Gymraeg Plasmawr

Poem Of A Child

This is a story of a child's life
One out of many others
One child and a happy story . . . and family
Or so it would seem.

For when she is in her room,
Or watching television, there will always be violence,
Everywhere she is, she is not safe
Never forget 'every tear tells a story'.

This child is never alone,
When her mother is out it starts then,
Her mother didn't see the danger she was in,
Her father on the other hand seemed to be ill.

This child is frightened when she is threatened,
But if she fights back she is in danger,
But what I don't see is,
Why doesn't she pick up the phone?

Actions may speak for words sometimes,
This is a story of a child's life,
There will always be violence,
She is never alone.

Never forget that actions speak for words,
Or that 'every tear tells a story'
We try to make it stop
But we can't do this without you!

Angharad Yorke (12)
Ysgol Gyfun Gymraeg Plasmawr

Away With Words

I wish I could go back in time
To let everybody know
How much I loved the world's great words
And didn't want them to go.

Goodbye words
I'll miss you so
Goodbye dear words
Please don't go

Now my hearing is gone
And I can no longer speak
Using actions to communicate
Every day of every week

Goodbye words
I'll miss you so
Goodbye dear words
Please don't go.

Holly Mileham (12)
Ysgol Gyfun Gymraeg Plasmawr

Autumn She Comes In Colours

Autumn's always changing
Mostly what she's wearing
Forever trying on different shades and colours
But never satisfied with the way she looks

Her moods are always changing too
She's very complex
She screams at the thunder and it bellows back
She throws things around in an angry rage
Until the trees beg her to stop, afraid of losing their leaves

When she's happy, everyone gets to hear about it
She'll paint the sky vibrant yellows, reds and browns
And perhaps a few splashes of pink here and there
Sometimes when autumn is bored, she calls upon her friend
The mischievous wind, and they laugh as they watch people
Chase after their hats and umbrellas

Autumn is very stylish. She wears the mist and the fog, like a
cashmere shawl
And sparkling spiderwebs like diamonds draped around her
Wearing gorgeous mahogany, ambers and of course her favourite
colour, glistening gold
A new outfit every day!
Autumn doesn't like the heat, that's why she and summer don't get on
But neither does she like the cold

But all too soon her beauty fades and she's struck by sadness
At the close of late November, Winter awakens
And it's time for her to leave
Her work done, her time over
Until next year she thinks . . .

Sarah Macgregor (13)
Ysgol Gyfun Gymraeg Plasmawr

Speedboating

Out there
Wind in your hair
Sun in your eyes
The world looks so wide

Away with the words
Emotions run free
Feelings are as a book
Open but no words

Gentle sounds
The sea, the engine
But none a human's
None a word

Overwhelming fun
Raining emotions
Feeling, sight and hearing
But no words

Words go with the wind
When speedboating.

Elin Salisbury (13)
Ysgol Gyfun Gymraeg Plasmawr

Away With Words

How can I explain
My feelings towards you?
You don't even look at me
Haven't a clue
I freeze when I see you
Don't know what to say
One look at your perfect face
Takes my breath away
Away with words!
I don't care
Let them look
Let them stare
And I'm always in competition
With the 'real men'
Just 'cause they can do a million press-ups
And I can only do ten
'Out of your league'
My friends all said
They never supported me once
Just laughed at me instead
Getting humiliated is worth it
If it means I'll get you
Things like these are worth it
Things I can get through
I hope you read this note
So you can see my other side
I'm not the coward you took me for
This time I won't hide
Away with words
Because I love you.

Thomas Mace (14)
Ysgol Gyfun Gymraeg Plasmawr

An Autumn Night

School's finally over for the day
A nightmare of a day it has been
In the car, a few hours later
Off to the place I love the most

Breathing in the soft smell
Feeling the touch of the horses' soft coats
My breathing slow down
A sense of calm around them

As I stroke the velvety nose
Of a bay horse that I will be riding
He nuzzles me with his nose
A kindness that cannot be found easily

I mount him and take the reins
He tosses his head, eager to go
Floating across the sandy arena
My troubles now forgotten

The rhythm of his trotting hooves
Warmth of his long back
The radio playing in the background
Brings some sense of calm to my mind

Now cantering smoothly round and round
A jump set in the middle of the arena
His stride lengthens
Clearing the fence with ease

I later take him to his field
His gentle breathing soothing
I let myself forget
It's just me and him

I let him off and as he canters I whisper, 'Goodbye Jacko'
He turns, neighs goodbye back and disappears into the darkness.

Hannah Brown (14)
Ysgol Gyfun Gymraeg Plasmawr

Away With Words

Let me show you
The love by
Helping people to show
How much I care
To clean the house, to show
My love to you is clean
I recycle to show concern
I always give people a second chance
I care for animals to show
I have softness in me
I protect people to show
I am strong

You don't need words to show
Your love for someone.

Megan Aur Lewis (13)
Ysgol Gyfun Gymraeg Plasmawr

Friendship

A friend is like an angel
Caring and unique
But also as we know
They are hard to seek

Friendship helps your happiness grow
And divides your sorrows
Something we treasure
Forever and ever and ever

Friends are a lucky wish
A rainbow for when you are blue
They're angels lifting your spirits up
When you most need them to

A friend is someone close to the heart
Even if we are apart
We shall stay friends forever
Because friendship is a true art.

Savanna Jones (13)
Ysgol Gyfun Gymraeg Plasmawr

I Love You

I love it when you're always there
I love the way you cut your hair
I love it when you always care
I love the way you look and stare
I love it when you make me shy
I love it when you make me cry
I love the fact this love is true
I love the fact I'd die for you!

Elin Jones (13)
Ysgol Gyfun Gymraeg Plasmawr

Heaven's Twilight

The sun sets in the autumn sky
Hills darken with fire-coloured forests at their feet

Leaves flutter to the floor
Adding to the already thick carpet
Tall trees create nature's cathedral
With a tawny-mahogany-amber roof

Cascades of copper fall from the oaks
Along with showers of buttercup-yellow and rusty-red
A gentle crunch accompanies your footfall

Mist enveloped the forest like a cloak
Impossible to shrug off
Spiderwebs become the most desirable silk, along with diamond droplets

Why do people rush to the Mediterranean
When all this is at their doorsteps?

Angharad Goode (13)
Ysgol Gyfun Gymraeg Plasmawr

My First Day At Primary School

'M um! Will I be alright in school?'
'Y es dear, why should you not be?'

F irst day nerves maybe?
I am quite scared of going to school
R ead books and get clever soon
S tart to enjoy your new school
T ime it will take time for you to settle in

D ad is not here to see me go to school either
A ccording to Dad he will pick me up from school
Y es, Dad you're here. 'How was school son?' 'Oh, it was amazing.'

Thomas Sims-Hayes (11)
Ysgol Gyfun Gymraeg Plasmawr

My First Day

I am confused
This large building where big boys live
Looms above me like a lion
Hunting the little children for desserts!

Teachers all around me
Their false grins and their eyes, striking me like daggers
While mine search for a friendly face
Hey! Wait a minute, where's my mum?

As the day goes by, the walls close in on me
The ceiling lower and lower
I feel a leak down below
And then another, a little higher up

Then it changes . . .

Jokes all day with my new friends
And playing on the concrete
I'm quite glad the day is over
. . . What? I have to go back tomorrow?

Iwan Hughes (11)
Ysgol Gyfun Gymraeg Plasmawr

My First Day At Primary School

M y first day at primary school was very scary,
'Y ou will make loads of new friends,' Mum said

F eeling scared I leave Mum crying
I go over to see some of the other girls
R unning from different classes
S eeing all these different people
T hey all look so odd, like aliens

D ay after day, I wake up really early and put on a uniform
A fter a week or so I settled in more,
'Y ou see, I told you it wouldn't be that bad,' said Mum.

Megan Eames (11)
Ysgol Gyfun Gymraeg Plasmawr

My First Day At Primary School

M onday the fifth of September 1999, my first day in nursery
Y ellow, the sickly colour of my childminder's aprons

F ighting, what most of the other kids were doing
I mpossible, it was impossible to get from one end of the room to
the other

R eady, I poised myself to let go of my mother's hand
S ulking, most of the other kids were!
T otal chaos. It was like a battleground apart from that the kids were
armed with teeth, not AK-47s

D ad, he was at work
A ngels, the complete opposite of this lot!
Y es! The end of day bell, I was going home there allowing the teeth
marks on my arm to heal!

Casey Copestick (11)
Ysgol Gyfun Gymraeg Plasmawr

My First Day At Primary School

M y mother was astounded
Y es very amazed

F irst day at school!
I would never be ready
R ight from the beginning I was nervous
S o timid, so small
T he clock was ticking

D own to the time when I would clamber in the car
A nd my mum would drive away to my very first
Y ear at school.

Tomos Roblin (11)
Ysgol Gyfun Gymraeg Plasmawr

Away With Words

Never run away with words
It's the worst thing you can ever do
They do nothing other than what the word is
Here is what some words do

Run, the word 'run' it's a funny word
But it's not funny when you're on holiday
And they run everywhere run and run
When you're in the pool, he's always running

Pig, the word 'pig' almost sounds fat when you say it
They eat, eat and eat, scoffing food down all the time
In the bar it cost him an absolute fortune
So never run away with the word pig

Rhyme, I hate rhyming, I got a rhyming dictionary once
I already knew it all, at the end of every sentence a rhyme
And all the time I wish I could rhyme
So never run away with words.

Ben Sawyer (12)
Ysgol Gyfun Gymraeg Plasmawr

Crabbed Football And Hooligans

Crabbed football and hooligans
Cannot live together
Football is a beautiful game
Hooligans are what destroys it
Football is skill and glory
Hooligans are smashing and beating
Football is an amazing sport
Hooligans are a disaster
Football is trying and taking part
Hooligans care about winning or losing
Football is to be watched
Hooligans disagree they want to take part
In a violent way
Football is a ball in the net!
Hooligans prefer a ball through a window
Football is a game that gives dreams
Hooligans is booze, drugs - disaster
That's why football and hooligans
Cannot be together.

Daniel Sion (12)
Ysgol Gyfun Gymraeg Plasmawr

Why?

Why the dark?
Why the pain?
Why the fear
And the shame?

Why so lonely?
Why so cold?
Why so hated
And so bold?

Why the lies?
Why the madness?
Why the mourn
And the sadness?

Why so stupid?
Why so ugly?
Why do people
Smile so smugly?

Jessica Collins (12)
Ysgol Gyfun Gymraeg Plasmawr

Life

We all have a life,
I have mine and you have yours,
But life includes being born and dying
Nobody can help that and that's
Why I'm explaining to you . . .

Life isn't easy it's hard
You're always turning a new page
You need help along the way
Of life your friends will be there,
Your family too
You rely on them and they rely on you.

Have fun along the way
Because you're life is like a roller coaster
Day after day
Look after yourself
Your friends and family and enjoy the ride
Well my point is you only have one life
Don't ruin it!

Jessica Thomas (12)
Ysgol Gyfun Gymraeg Plasmawr

Witnesses

When Pompeii was burnt by a volcano,
Thousands died
There were witnesses
By the mountain edge
They couldn't make it
I was lucky,
I wasn't there.

When the Titanic sunk,
Thousands died
There were witnesses
On the ship's deck
They couldn't make it
I was lucky
I wasn't there.

When terrorists destroyed the World Trade Center
Thousands died
There were witnesses
Up the North Tower
They couldn't make it
I was lucky
I wasn't there.

When an earthquake hit Kashmir
Thousands died
There were witnesses
On the hilltops
They couldn't make it
I was lucky
I wasn't there.

When a tsunami hit Indonesia,
Thousands died
I was a witness
I was swimming in the sea
I couldn't make it
I wasn't so lucky
I was there.

Henri Williams (12)
Ysgol Gyfun Gymraeg Plasmawr

Away With Words

If there were no words
Only grunts and noises,
The only communication would be through
Signs and emotions.

If there were no words
Only pictures and photographs,
You could see what was happening
But not know where and how.

If there were no words
Only music and rhythm
The swarm of beautiful music,
But no words to express your feelings.

If there were no words
The world would be such a gloomy place,
But lucky for us
Our world is a better place.

Aled Bryn Williams (12)
Ysgol Gyfun Gymraeg Plasmawr

Away With Words

As the boat slows to a halt
All I can see is turquoise ocean
The rhythmic beat of waves on wood
Doesn't disturb my imagination
My pen touches the paper
And travels along the clean white page
Thoughts and feelings pour out
I couldn't stop them if I tried
The sun presses down on my eyes
So I close them and think for a while
The gentle rocking of the boat
Inspires me to write
So I reach for my faithful pen
And before long I have created
A whole new world
With my words and my ideas
Ready for someone else to read
And enjoy

Dela Anderson (12)
Ysgol Gyfun Gymraeg Plasmawr

The Disco

The people dancing
Laughing, screaming
The bright lights
Shining on them
Music pumping
Like thunder
Burgers sizzling
Thirst-quenching pop
DJ changing
The music
From R&B to rap
The people laughing
Screaming and
Having fun.

Rachel Hiatt (13)
Ysgol Gyfun Gymraeg Plasmawr

My First Day At Primary School

A long, long way from home
I walk through the doors holding Mummy, tight
So big, so noisy, so different
Mummy knocks at the door of my room
A woman answers
She must be the teacher
I start to cry
I don't want to let go of Mummy, never ever,

'Come and see your new friends,' says the teacher
I peep into the class
Why is everyone so happy?
I won't let go of Mummy, never ever
'Look there's that girl that lives on our street!'
Mummy said, so I start to walk up to her
She's doing a puzzle what's it called, oh yeah,
A jigsaw.

Mummy says goodbye
I give her a big cuddle,
'See you tonight!' says Mummy
When will tonight come?
It seems a long way away from now

I'm hot in this big jumper
Should I ask to take it off
Or just leave it on?
I don't know
I don't know anything
Will I be lost?
When will I see Mummy?
Why am I in school?

Mali Williams (11)
Ysgol Gyfun Gymraeg Plasmawr

My First Day At Primary School

In the playground people running round,
Bouncing up and down,
Why where they excited?
I don't like this!
It's going to be boring.

I walked through the big doors, or gate
Then my lunch box fell out of my bag
And landed in a puddle
Big people laughed at me
I cried
I got up and ran outside
Running behind me was a woman
The woman was yelling out words
I didn't understand
She looked angry but then smiled
And said, 'Ah, reception.'
And patted me on the head
She took me to my classroom
And told me to sit down and read a book
A book? What's a book?

Nia Williams (11)
Ysgol Gyfun Gymraeg Plasmawr

My First Day

M ummy's not here anymore
Y ellow bricks and paint make the school a sickly shade

F eeble, small, little me in a crowd of pushing kids
I feel smaller than ever now, entering the zoo
R ough kids barging past, no sympathy
S tumbling, falling into a world of the unknown,
' T oday you are going to school,' Mum said.

D id she know I would be this lost and confused?
A day ago, did I imagine this, as I topple over,
' Y ou, kid, your shoelace is untied!'

Hannah Smith (12)
Ysgol Gyfun Gymraeg Plasmawr

Young Writers Information

We hope you have enjoyed reading this book - and that you will continue to enjoy it in the coming years.

If you like reading and writing poetry drop us a line, or give us a call, and we'll send you a free information pack.

Alternatively if you would like to order further copies of this book or any of our other titles, then please give us a call or log onto our website at www.youngwriters.co.uk

**Young Writers Information
Remus House
Coltsfoot Drive
Peterborough
PE2 9JX**

(01733) 890066